1286

970.01    Sandak, Cass R.
SAN
          Columbus Day

$10.95

| DATE | | | |
|---|---|---|---|
| | | | |
| | | | |
| | | | |
| | | | |
| | | | |
| | | | |
| | | | |
| | | | |
| | | | |
| | | | |
| | | | |
| | | | |

# Columbus Day

### BY
## Cass R. Sandak

# CRESTWOOD HOUSE
### New York

**Library of Congress Cataloging-in-Publication Data**
Sandak, Cass R.
  Columbus Day

  p.    c.m.—(Holidays)
  Includes bibliographical references.
  Summary: Discusses why and how Columbus Day is celebrated and highlights the life and voyages of
the famous explorer.
   1. Columbus Day—Juvenile literature. 2. Columbus, Christopher—Juvenile literature. 3. America—
Discovery and exploration—Spanish—Juvenile literature. [1. Columbus Day. 2. Columbus, Christopher.
3. Explorers. 4. America—Discovery and exploration.]   I. Title. II. Series: Holidays.
E120.S25    1990        970.01'5—dc20        89-25399                               CIP
ISBN 0-89686-498-7                                                                   AC

**Photo Credits**
Cover: The Granger Collection
Culver Pictures, Inc.: 4, 10, 13, 16, 19, 20, 24, 26, 29, 30, 32, 35, 39, 41
AP—Wide World: 8
British Museum: 22
New York Public Library Picture Collection: 36
Frank Sloan: 43

Macmillan Publishing Company
866 Third Avenue
New York, NY 10022
Collier Macmillan Canada, Inc.

CRESTWOOD HOUSE

Printed in the United States

First Edition

10 9 8 7 6 5 4 3 2 1

# Contents

"He gained a world; he gave that world
Its grandest lesson: "On! Sail on!"
— Joaquin Miller

# A Big Parade

It could be said that the first Columbus Day celebration was held on March 15, 1493. On that day, Christopher Columbus returned to Spain from his voyage across the Atlantic Ocean. Crowds cheered and church bells tolled.

Columbus's journey had lasted almost a year. It had started and ended in the small port of Palos. From Palos, the homecoming parade traveled to Barcelona, 500 miles away. There, King Ferdinand and Queen Isabella were waiting to greet Columbus.

In each town the parade passed through, there were shouts of joy. People had been told of Columbus's great achievement. They stood in large crowds, trying to glimpse the famous man. Bands of musicians led the parade from one town to the next.

Columbus kneeling in front of the king and queen of Spain.     5

By mid-April, almost a month later, the group had reached Barcelona. The parade into the city was arranged in a special way. The six Indians Columbus had brought back from his trip came first. They carried some of the strange new foods and brilliantly colored birds that Columbus had found in the New World. Next came the crews of the ships. Columbus followed, on a white horse. His sons walked beside him. The younger, Fernando, was only five.

When he got to the royal canopy under which the king and queen of Spain sat, Columbus displayed all the strange new plants, precious jewels, and gold he had brought. He explained about the American natives. He told who they were and how kind they had been to him and his men. And he told the king and queen about his achievements.

It was a thrilling and triumphant event. From that moment on, Columbus was a hero.

# Making Columbus Day a National Holiday

Three hundred years later, Columbus was again given a day of celebration. The first "official" Columbus Day was held on October 12, 1792. This was the day the explorer actually landed in the New World. October 12 was kept as the holiday until 1971. In that year, the U.S. government changed the date to the Monday nearest October 12.

This first large Columbus Day celebration was held in New York City on October 12, 1792. A group known as the Columbian Order gave a special dinner. The dinner was followed by speeches and elaborate ceremonies. They also set up a temporary monument in the society's headquarters. At the time it was the only statue of Columbus in the United States. For the nation's 100th birthday in 1876, a permanent statue was put up in Philadelphia's Fairmount Park.

There were no more Columbus Days until 1892. In that year, President Benjamin Harrison issued a proclamation. He wanted a special national celebration to honor the 400th anniversary of Columbus's landing. He asked Congress to finance a World's Fair to be known as the Columbian Exposition. It would be held in Chicago. He declared October 12, 1892, a national holiday.

Because this celebration was such a huge project, the fair didn't open until May 1, 1893. It was very popular. Millions of visitors came from around the country and from all over the world. They came to see the fair grounds, with its collection of fine buildings.

A special coin, featuring the face of Queen Isabella, was issued for the exposition. It was the only time a U.S. coin displayed the image of a foreign ruler. It was also at the Columbian Exposition that the Pledge of Allegiance to the flag was introduced.

Some people wanted to make October 12 a national holiday. Many Italian-Americans supported this idea. After all, Columbus had been born in Italy.

In 1882, a society of the Roman Catholic Church was formed to promote friendship among its members. Its name was the Knights of Columbus. This group wanted Columbus's name to be famous.

In 1905, the governor of Colorado asked for the day to be a legal holiday. In 1906, the mayor of Chicago made a similar request. New York Governor Charles Evans Hughes vetoed (turned down) the request in his state in 1908, however. He felt there was little demand

for such a celebration. But the veto caused a lot of protests. Wisely, Hughes changed his mind and signed the law creating the holiday on March 23, 1909. In New York State, the holiday became a legal one.

On October 12, 1909, replicas of Columbus's ships, the *Niña, Pinta,* and *Santa Maria* sailed slowly up New York Harbor. The ships were joined by American and Italian warships. Great crowds and booming cannons saluted the vessels. On that same day, many Italian-Americans marched in a parade. They went up New York City's Fifth Avenue as far as Columbus Circle. A column topped by a statue of Columbus had guarded the southwest entrance to Central Park since 1892. As part of the celebration, the governor addressed members of the Knights of Columbus at Carnegie Hall.

In 1910, Boston named Columbus Day a legal holiday and held its first Columbus Day parade. President William Howard Taft was there, too. It was the longest parade in Boston's history.

State by state, the holiday was accepted, and in 1934 President Franklin D. Roosevelt issued a proclamation asking all 48 states to observe October 12 as a national holiday, Columbus Day. In a few states, the day was known until recently as Landing Day or Discovery Day.

# Columbus Day Everywhere

Except for religious holidays, Columbus Day is the only holiday all countries in North and South America celebrate together. The day is

A marching band and flag bearers lead a modern Columbus Day parade.

also celebrated in Puerto Rico. Puerto Ricans feel especially proud that Columbus discovered their island on his second voyage. The holiday is also observed in some parts of Canada. In some places in both Spain and Italy, there are church ceremonies, parades, and fireworks.

Even though Columbus was Italian, he made his voyage for Spain. The Spanish, therefore, celebrate October 12 as well. In Barcelona, Spain, there is a 90-foot-long model of the *Santa Maria*. An outdoor pageant is performed with as many as 2,000 spectators watching.

To most of us, Columbus Day means parades. Many American cities have them. In 1957, Boston held a celebration that lasted three days! A typical Columbus Day parade in Los Angeles begins with the Italian flag and the Stars and Stripes flying side by side over City Hall. All-day celebrations include parades of floats and bands playing both Italian and American music. Evening activities include banquets and balls with important guests. New York City's Columbus Day parade traces a route very much like those taken by earlier marchers. Many people who take part in the parade are Italian Americans. Recent marshals of parades have included such noted Italians as Sophia Loren and opera singer Luciano Pavarotti.

# Before Columbus

Before the 1400s, few sailors had ventured out into the Atlantic Ocean. No one had any idea how big the ocean was. No one even thought that there was land to the west. The Muslims referred to the Atlantic Ocean as the Green Sea of Darkness. They were so terrified of the ocean that they felt people who sailed on it were crazy.

At Columbus Day parades during World War II, Italian-American women carried flags in honor of the soldiers in their families.

Ancient peoples liked the warm safety of the Mediterranean Sea. Some Phoenician sailors, however, had ventured out into the Atlantic. They sailed through the Gates of Hercules and out into the Atlantic. By 1100 B.C., they had founded a settlement at present-day Cadiz, Spain, north of Gibraltar. Around 325 B.C. a Greek mariner traveled even further. A man named Pytheas sailed to the British Isles and possibly even to Scandinavia. Roman ships regularly sailed as far as the British Isles, too. Many historians believe that an Irish monk named Saint Brendan traveled westward to unidentified places in the Atlantic Ocean in the 6th century A.D.

The most important explorers into the Atlantic before Columbus were the Vikings. Around A.D. 800 Vikings (or Norsemen) set out to find new homes. They were good sailors. Their boats were long, narrow and open. Around 850, the Vikings settled Iceland. In about 982, Eric the Red discovered and explored Greenland. He set up colonies there that lasted for several hundred years. From Greenland, other mariners sailed farther west. In about A.D. 1000 they discovered a place they called Vinland. It is thought that Leif Ericsson, the son of Eric the Red, found and named Vinland.

No one knows for sure just where Vinland was. Places on the Atlantic coast of North America from Newfoundland to Virginia have all been suggested. Today people think that Vinland was somewhere along the southern coast of New England. Like Columbus, Leif Ericsson was a discoverer of North America. And in several places in the United States, a day to honor Leif Ericsson is also celebrated.

The Viking voyages did not lead to any permanent settlements in North America. But stories of Ericsson's adventures spread through Europe and probably reached the ears of the young Christopher Columbus.

Vikings crossed the Atlantic to explore the New World 600 years before Columbus did.

# The Young Columbus

No one is sure exactly when Christopher Columbus was born. The best guesses place the date between August 25 and October 31. Most people agree that the year was 1451. Born in Italy, Columbus had an Italian name: Cristoforo Colombo. Christopher Columbus is the English version of his name.

Even where he was born in Italy is not certain. Sixteen cities have claimed to be Columbus's birthplace! But one seems to be the most probable: Genoa, a major port on the Mediterranean Sea. Today there is an inscription on the little house where people believe Columbus was born:

> No house is more to be honored
> than this where Christopher
> Columbus spent his early youth.

Columbus's father's name was Domenico. His mother's name was Susanna. Most likely, they were both wool weavers. Columbus had several brothers and sisters, including Bartholomew, who was slightly younger.

Because Genoa was an active trading city, young Christopher probably heard exciting stories from sailors in the local harbor. He must have known about the voyages of people looking for new trade routes.

His father taught him how to weave, but the boy didn't like the work. There is no record of Columbus having had any formal education. He probably never even went to school. He ran away to sea, possibly when he was only 14. In 1474 or 1475, when Columbus was in his early twenties, he hired himself out as a sailor. The ship was going to Chios, an island east of mainland Greece.

By the time Columbus was 25, he had become a sailor on a ship bound for Portugal. The ship was wrecked in a storm, and Columbus was left floating in the water. He clung to a floating oar for support, prayed, and then began to swim the six miles to shore. Miraculously he made it and then headed for Lisbon.

In those days, Portuguese merchants and sailors were leaders in navigation. They wanted to find new trade routes. Prince Henry of Portugal had been a key figure in making Portugal the world leader in exploration. He was known as Prince Henry the Navigator. The Portuguese were looking for a way to sail around Africa. This would lead them to the Far East and its riches of spices, silk, and gold. But even in the 1470s, when Columbus arrived in Lisbon, no one had yet sailed the full length of Africa. At least, no one had lived to return and tell about it.

# A Man with a Dream

Columbus had set sail for Portugal to find his brother Bartholomew, who made maps, globes, and charts. These weren't the maps and globes we know today, for no one knew what the world really looked like. Some of the globes were egg-shaped, cylindrical, or pear-shaped. A few were even round. Most maps just showed Europe and the Atlantic Ocean. Some showed parts of Africa and Asia with the Indies far to the left. But no one had guessed even that there was another continent out there.

Nor could people agree on the shape of the world. Many learned people, including Aristotle and the Greeks of the 4th century B.C., believed that the world was round. An Italian astronomer, Paolo

Toscanelli, had drawn a map showing that India could be reached by sailing due west across the Atlantic. But in Columbus's time, only a few people held this belief. Columbus was one of those few. He was the first to prove it was true.

Despite his fame, no one knows for sure what Columbus looked like. The earliest painting of Columbus dates from 1575—and the man had been dead for 70 years by then! The only descriptions we have of him are words put down by Columbus's son, Fernando. Columbus is described as being about 5′10″, and having blue eyes and a hooked nose. His hair was sandy to red, but it had turned white before Columbus was thirty. By all accounts he was a very religious man and remained so all his life.

Henry the Navigator, the prince who inspired Portuguese sailors to become the leading explorers of their day.

PRINCE HENRY
OF
PORTUGALL

Columbus was not well educated as a child. He only knew the language that the people in Genoa spoke. There is some doubt whether he could read or write before he was in his twenties.

Columbus was very smart. While he was in Lisbon, he realized he needed to learn to read and write. He would have to read navigational charts and keep naval logs. He learned both Portuguese and Spanish. Columbus began to investigate astronomy and mathematics. He also studied Latin, the language used by all learned people of the time. He realized that he would need to know many things if he wanted to achieve his goals.

At about the same time, Columbus probably came across the most famous travel book of all time, *The Travels of Marco Polo*. He read about the exciting adventures of Marco, his father, and uncle. They had journeyed to the Far East in the 1200s and wrote an account of their trip. These tales inspired Columbus to pursue his dream of finding a path to the riches of the Far East.

In 1476, Columbus sailed to Ireland. There he probably heard about Saint Brendan's voyage. A year later Columbus made a voyage north to Iceland. And there he probably learned about the Viking exploits of four hundred years earlier.

In 1478, Columbus married Felipa Moniz de Perestrello. She was a wealthy and well-born Portuguese lady. A year later, Felipa gave birth to their son, Diego. They spent much of their time in the Madeira Islands, near the coast of Portugal. During this period, Columbus learned even more about the latest navigation methods. And he thought about sailing ships westward across the Atlantic Ocean.

This was not a totally new idea, and Columbus had studied it carefully. If, as he believed, the world was round, it made perfect sense. If he sailed due west, he would eventually reach the Indies. At that time, the Indies included Japan, China, and India, as well as the East Indies. These exotic places were the home of silks, spices, and jewels. As Columbus's knowledge grew, so did his self-confidence. He would never be able to afford the journey on his own, however. Full of enthusiasm, he began to look for someone to provide the money for the long trip.

The search would last for fourteen years.

# Columbus Looks for a Patron

The first person Columbus turned to was a great-nephew of Prince Henry the Navigator. He was King John II of Portugal. Columbus asked him for a crew and a fleet of ships to make a westward journey to the Indies. Columbus made a tempting promise. He would find a route that would make Portugal the richest and most powerful of all countries. Any new lands the explorer discovered would be claimed for Portugal. John II took a year to make up his mind. He then turned Columbus down.

At about the same time, Columbus's wife died. Columbus was left to take care of their son, Diego. He and Diego traveled to Spain and went to La Rabida, a monastery not far from the sea coast. In Spain, Columbus hoped to ask the king and queen for money for the journey.

Columbus and his son stayed at La Rabida for several weeks. Columbus talked with the monks there about his plan to sail westward and his need for money. The monks decided to pray for him. Then

The earliest and probably the most accurate portrait of Christopher Columbus. It was painted by Sir Antonio Moro, a famous court artist, 70 years after Columbus's death.

Columbus, his sons, and an unidentified woman in a drawing done in 1794.

a priest—who sometimes served as a chaplain to the queen — heard about Columbus's plan. He agreed to speak with the queen about Columbus's voyage.

The king and queen of Spain were Ferdinand of Aragon and Isabella of Castile. Their marriage had linked two kingdoms of Spain into one great nation. Columbus also met a man named Don Luis de Santagel. As it turned out, Santagel was the Budget Minister for the Spanish crown. Santagel presented Columbus to Queen Isabella in 1486.

Both Ferdinand and Isabella liked Columbus's idea. The queen even formed a committee to consider Columbus's plan. But, the two monarchs were busy building a united Spain. They were engaged in a war to drive the Moors, or Muslims, out of Spain. The Moors had been in Spain for about 700 years. For a time they had dominated the country. Even though Ferdinand and Isabella liked Columbus's idea, they had little time and almost no money to devote to the project.

Two years later, in 1488, Columbus's brother Bartholomew tried to get the kings of both England and France to finance the trip. Both attempts failed. That same year Columbus's second son, Fernando, was born to Beatriz Enriquez de Harana, a Spanish woman.

Columbus approached the Spanish monarchs again and again, but they kept turning him down. Then in January 1492, Ferdinand and Isabella were at last able to rid Spain of the Moors. At Granada, the leaders of the Muslim armies finally surrendered. The king and queen could now turn their attention to Columbus.

Columbus didn't know any of this. Discouraged, he was about to leave Spain when he received a summons to return to the court. Finally! Ferdinand and Isabella approved Columbus's plan and agreed to back his adventure. They believed the voyage would advance trade. They were also eager to spread the Christian religion to new lands.

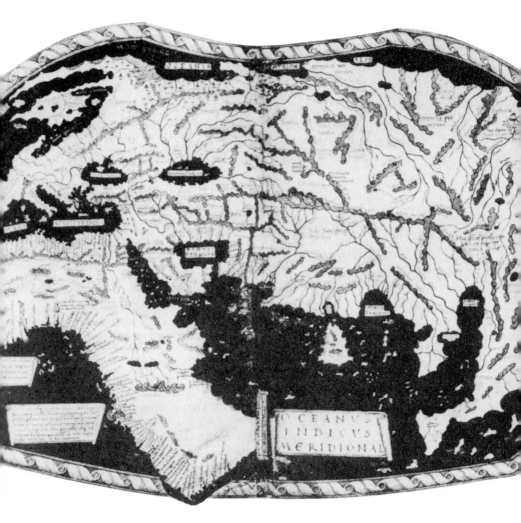

A map of the world as it was known before Columbus's first
voyage.

Columbus asked for — and got — good terms for his voyage. He would be named "Admiral of the Ocean Seas." He would also be appointed governor of any lands he discovered. He would receive one tenth of all the gems, gold, and silver he found. The king and queen provided Columbus with enough money to pay his crew for four months. They also gave him an official letter of introduction to the emperor of China. After all, China was Columbus's destination. He was to present the document when he arrived at the Chinese court.

# The *Niña,* the *Pinta,* and the *Santa Maria*

The king and queen of Spain agreed to give Columbus two ships for his journey. These were to be caravels, a kind of sailing ship. Columbus himself would provide a third ship. These were the three vessels the world has come to know as the *Niña*, the *Pinta*, and the *Santa Maria*.

No one is sure exactly what the ships were like. The *Santa Maria* was probably the largest of the three. It was the one in which Columbus sailed. Juan de la Cosa, the owner of the *Santa Maria*, was also aboard. The ship was about 90 feet long and held the largest crew. It was also the slowest ship.

The hull was constructed of rough wood held together by iron nails. Although the hull was painted with tar, water could still seep in. The ship carried weapons, food, and supplies for a year, and goods to

The *Santa Maria* (left) flew a flag emblazoned with the initials of the Spanish monarchs—I and F.

barter. All of this was stored in the hold, at the bottom of the ship.

There was simple galley (or kitchen) where the food was prepared. However, the food quickly spoiled and was in bad condition due to heat and the damp. Meat and fish were salted to keep them from spoiling. Cheeses were soon riddled with red worms. Flour and bread became moldy or full of bugs. Fresh fruits and vegetables were only available during the first few days of the voyage. Fresh water kept in barrels soon turned slimy.

Columbus's cabin was on an upper deck at the rear of the ship. It was large and contained a bed, a dining table, and chairs for two people. There was even a closet. Columbus's equipment — compass, charts, books, and astrolabe — was also in his cabin. The compass allowed Columbus to know which direction was north. He could do this day and night and in all kinds of weather. The astrolabe helped Columbus determine the position of stars in the sky.

The crew kept time by hour glasses. When the hour was gone, the glasses were turned over and the next hour was counted. Half the crew worked while the other half slept. Everyone served in four-hour shifts, or watches. Since there was not much sleeping space on the ships, this was a practical solution.

The *Niña* and the *Pinta* were smaller than the *Santa Maria*. *Niña* was a nickname meaning "baby." The ship's full name was *Santa Clara*. *Pinta* was also a nickname, meaning "painted lady." What the *Pinta's* full name was has never been discovered. The *Niña* was about 70 feet long. The *Pinta*, at 56 feet, was slightly smaller. All three boats were made of wood and carried sails. These sails enabled the ships to sail either with, or into, the wind.

Martin Alonso Pinzon was the captain of the *Pinta*, and his brother Vicente Pinzon was the commander of the *Niña*. The owner of the

Columbus and his crew prepared to set sail from the port of Palos, Spain on August 3, 1492.

*Pinta* also went along, but only as a passenger. Besides sailors, a doctor and a surgeon were also on board. These were not like the doctors and surgeons we know today. They were crudely trained seamen who could only treat some types of wounds. They were also able to saw off a limb if an injury became infected.

About 120 sailors made up the crew. Seventy men were on the *Santa Maria*, and about 25 each were on the smaller ships. Some reports indicate that the crews may have been made up of prisoners. They would be pardoned of their crimes if they sailed on this voyage. Other reports indicate that the sailors were all experienced. They wanted the fame and money that would come with the trip.

By royal agreement, Columbus was to get his fleet ready as quickly as possible. It took several months longer than expected, however. On the morning of August 3, 1492, the three ships were ready. At the dock, crowds of family members wept and priests chanted. The tiny fleet finally left the Spanish port of Palos and headed for the sea. No one knew if they would ever return.

# The Voyage Begins

Although they were considered modern in 1492, Columbus's ships did not offer much in the way of comfort, safety, or hygiene. Life on board was uncomfortable. There was no ice or refrigeration to keep food fresh. Insects and rats ran over the ships. Navigational instruments were simple. The only communication between the three ships was done by their lanterns.

The fleet sailed west. In about a week, they arrived at the Canary Islands, 700 miles away. During the stop, the crew changed the ships' sails. Round sails were used in the Mediterranean. Square ones would be needed on the rougher and wilder Atlantic. They also repaired the *Pinta's* broken rudder before sailing on in early September.

Columbus was a skilled sailor, knowledgeable in many areas. But many of the crew were ignorant and superstitious. They expected to find sea monsters and demons out on the Atlantic. There were rumors that the waters of the Atlantic boiled. People also said there was a mysterious black fog that engulfed everything. Some thought monstrous animals would rise up out of the churning ocean to destroy the sailors and their ships.

On the trip, Columbus kept two sets of records. In one of them, he kept a log in which he recorded navigational data and official weather and ship reports that all could see. In the other, Columbus wrote down his personal thoughts about what was happening each day. These secret reports were not made public.

By mid-September the ships were in the middle of the Sargasso Sea, a section of the Atlantic near Bermuda. This part of the journey was slowed considerably by masses of seaweed. This seaweed clogs the waters in this portion of the Atlantic. The weary sailors often thought they had sighted land. Two sightings turned out to be only cloud banks. Flocks of migrating birds flying overhead also made them think land was near. But it wasn't. Soon after leaving the Sargasso Sea, the unhappy crew began to talk of mutiny and rebellion.

# Land Ahoy!

Then, just when everyone had given up hope, land was sighted. On the evening of October 11, Columbus was certain he saw a light of some sort flickering in the distance. Then, at two in the morning on

On October 11, 1492, Columbus stood on the deck of his ship and got his first look at the New World.

Columbus and his shipmates thank God for their safe passage across the Atlantic.

October 12, 1492, Rodrigo de Triana, a lookout on the *Pinta*, shouted that he saw land! He was the first European to see what we now know as the Americas.

At daybreak, Columbus and some of the crew climbed into a small rowboat to get a closer look at the land. Columbus was dressed in a purple cloak. He carried a flag from Spain and a cross. When he stepped from the boat, he knelt and planted the flag and the cross firmly in the sand. He then claimed the land for Spain. The cross had a large *F* on one side and an *I* on the other. The letters were the initials of the Spanish monarchs who had made the trip possible.

Where was this landing? Most scholars agree that the Bahama Islands, just south of Florida, was the likely place. Columbus named the spot San Salvador, or Holy Savior.

What no one can be sure of today is which one of the Bahamas was the site of Columbus's first landing. There are over 3,000 islands and cays (small islands) in the Bahamas. For many years people assumed that Watling Island was the spot. A plaque there reads:

> On this spot Christopher
> Columbus first set foot on the
> soil of the New World.

Recent findings, however, suggest that Samana Cay was the place where Columbus first set foot in the New World. Scientists have found relics from Spanish ships at Samana Cay.

What did Columbus find? Columbus and his crew had expected to land on the edge of Asia. After all, they had sailed west for a month. Wasn't the Far East where they *should* have been?

The people who came out to meet Columbus were not Asians. They were dark-skinned members of a Carib Indian tribe, possibly the Arawak. These people were not warlike, but instead were gentle and helpful. In fact, Columbus took several of the Caribs with him

Columbus leaving his fleet to explore the coast of Cuba on his
second voyage.

when he left San Salvador a few days later. The crew had refreshed themselves and loaded a new supply of fresh water onto the ships. Columbus saw San Salvador only as a stopping-off place. He still believed he and his ships were just off the shore of India and the Far East.

On the 18th of October, just a few days later, the fleet came to Cuba. Columbus could tell this was a big island, and he was sure it must be either Japan or mainland China.

On this part of the trip, Columbus saw two important Indian inventions. The Indians used small, light boats to get from place to place. They called these boats canoes. At another place he spotted Indians sleeping in slinglike beds strung between two trees. Columbus adapted these beds, which he then put on his ships. They let sailors sleep comfortably in small spaces and kept them dry. We know them as hammocks.

Some of the new foods that Columbus found included sweet potatoes, corn (maize), and pumpkins. The Caribs made cassava bread from the tapioca plant. Columbus and his men probably also saw tobacco plants growing. They saw people smoking a dried tobacco leaf rolled up and lighted. It was an early form of cigarette.

In November, Martin Pinzon and the *Pinta* left the little fleet and went off in search of gold. In early December the *Niña* and *Santa Maria* reached the Caribbean island now known as Hispaniola. On the day before Christmas, the *Santa Maria* ran aground. It was destroyed.

All was not lost, however. On Christmas morning, Caribs helped the crew save almost everything from the ship — even the timbers. Because the two smaller ships couldn't carry all the crew, 43 men were left behind. They lived in a shelter made with timbers from the wrecked vessel. Columbus left behind food to last them for a year.

Because he was a religious man, Columbus saw this event as a sign from God. He called the settlement La Navidad, the Spanish word for Christmas.

On January 4, 1493, the return voyage began. Besides the crew, Columbus took several other passengers on board including several natives and colorful birds and parrots. Because Columbus was convinced that San Salvador was part of the Indies, he called the people he found living there Indians. The name caught on. Columbus hoped to convert them to Christianity. He was also fascinated by the gold ornaments they wore!

# The Second Voyage

We have already seen how triumphantly Columbus was received when he returned to Spain. Ferdinand and Isabella were delighted with the results of Columbus's first voyage. They were even more anxious to make plans for a second journey. Preparations were finished in record time.

On September 25, 1493, a second ship called the *Santa Maria* took Columbus out of the Spanish harbor of Cadiz. Eleven other ships set out on the voyage. This was the largest fleet Columbus was ever to command. The purpose of this voyage was to make Christians out of the natives in the Indies. And there would be plenty of time for some new exploring as well.

The expedition landed first at the island now named Saint Croix. It continued on to the island of Puerto Rico. Then the sailors returned to La Navidad, the place where Columbus had left the men from the previous voyage. But the news there was not good. Many of the sailors had fought among themselves and killed each other. Some thought

An artist's idea of what the first Christian service in the Americas
34    may have looked like.

Columbus found Venezuela—and natives diving for pearls—on his third voyage.

they might even have been murdered by unfriendly Indians. Columbus then sailed on to Jamaica. He didn't leave to go home again until March 1496.

Word of the Spanish rebellion at La Navidad may have reached the queen and king. Whatever the reason, they became less enthusiastic about Columbus's ventures. Although he was eager to begin a third voyage, the king and queen did not give him their immediate approval.

# The Third and Fourth Voyages

On May 30, 1498, however, a fleet of six ships sailed once more from Spain. By the end of July, Columbus was again in the Caribbean Sea. This time his major discovery was an island he named Trinidad (which means Trinity in English). The group sailed on and landed on the northwest coast of South America, in what we now know as Venezuela. Columbus was again convinced he was in some part of Asia. He never was to learn that he had touched South America.

After a short stay there, Columbus and his ships sailed to Hispaniola (Little Spain) where a small Spanish colony had been established. He reached Santo Domingo (now the capital of the Dominican Republic). There he found chaos. Columbus did what he could to restore order. But, reports accused Columbus of crimes against the settlers and against the native Indians. These reports reached the king and queen in Spain. They sent a representative, Francisco Bobadilla, to look into the rumors of Columbus's misdoings.

When he arrived in Santo Domingo, Bobadilla seized control of the island. He placed Columbus under arrest. The famous explorer was shipped back to Spain in chains. At the Spanish court, Columbus was able to prove his innocence. It is said that the story of Columbus's plight moved Queen Isabella to tears. The explorer was pardoned. Once more, the king and queen and the Spanish thought well of the hero. But the whole affair left a lasting impression on Columbus. He requested that his iron chains be buried with him. No one knows whether they were or not.

Isabella and Ferdinand gave Columbus another chance. His fourth and last voyage began in 1502. The ships sailed past some of the islands the Spaniards had landed on in the past. Columbus was still determined to reach India. This time he and his sailors discovered the region we know as Central America and sailed along the coast of Honduras.

It was during this voyage that the famous story about Columbus and the eclipse of the sun occurred. Columbus and several of his men were being held captive by the Indians. Desperate to get themselves released, Columbus used his cunning. From his studies of astronomy, he knew that there was soon to be an eclipse of the sun. The natives had no idea what was going to happen. Columbus was able to convince them that he had performed a kind of magic. This magic turned the sun dark in the middle of the day. The Indians were impressed and released all the prisoners.

Aboard ship again, the sailors encountered a bad storm. They changed their course and sailed on toward the east. They arrived at Jamaica and landed there. Columbus spent almost a year in Jamaica before sailing for Spain. In November 1504, he was back in Spain — for the last time.

By that time Queen Isabella was dangerously ill. Within three weeks of Columbus's return, she died. When she died, the last support

Columbus won freedom from his native captors when he convinced them he had the power to darken the sun.

for Columbus died as well. Ferdinand turned his back on the explorer. The king even denied Columbus the rewards that had been promised him.

Columbus died soon after, on May 20, 1506. He was buried, with little ceremony, in Seville, Spain. But the wandering man's bones didn't rest. In 1542, his remains—along with those of one of his sons—were sent to Santo Domingo. The people of Santo Domingo wanted to honor him. In 1877, while the cathedral there was being repaired, a coffin was unearthed. It bore the inscription, "Illustrious and noble man, Christopher Columbus." The coffin was believed to contain the remains of Columbus's body. And, in 1892, a monument was erected to Columbus in the Santo Domingo cathedral.

# The Legacy of Columbus

Columbus has left us with one of the earliest and most exciting of all adventure stories. His reasoning was sound, even if his sense of distance wasn't.

Among Columbus's most lasting achievements are the incredible variety of new foods he found in the New World and brought back with him to Europe. These included corn, beans, tomatoes, pine-apple, green pepper, strawberries, avocados, papayas, and peanuts.

There are hundreds, if not thousands, of places named after this great explorer. Oddly enough, Columbus's name was not given to either of the two continents he found in the New World. But Colum-

A mapmaker as well as explorer, Columbus charted his course across the Atlantic.

bus did give his name to a variety of rivers, cities, state capitals, and towns. Our nation's capital is the District of Columbia. Schools and universities were named after him. Colombia, in South America, Columbus Circle in New York City, and the space shuttle, *Columbia*, all bear witness to the explorer's fame. The Pan American Building in Washington, D.C., contains the Columbus Memorial Library. In the library are official documents from the 21 American republics that make up North, Central, and South America. In 1984, the city of Columbus, Ohio, honored Columbus by installing a 7,000-lb. 20-foot-high statue of the explorer.

Columbus went to his grave never knowing exactly what he had discovered. To the end, he remained convinced that he had gone west to get to the East. He was sure he had found the fabled kingdoms of Asia. How could he have known that instead he had discovered a New World?

Columbus's statue guards an entrance to New York City's Central Park.

# Columbus Day Trivia

There is a legend that says Columbus wasn't the *first* member of his crew to land in the New World but the second. How could this be? The story says that a young crew member from the *Santa Maria*, an Irish lad named Patrick McGuire, was so eager to precede Columbus that he stepped off the small boat that was bringing them to shore. He did this, the story says, so that McGuire could lay his coat down so Columbus wouldn't get his feet wet. It's a good story, but what was an Irishman doing on a Spanish boat with an Italian captain?

### Two Riddles

Q: Why did some people think Columbus wasn't very bright?

A: Because he didn't know where he was going, where he had been, or where he was when he got there.

Q: Which two state capital names begin with the same first six letters? (Hint: Both were named after Columbus.)

A: Columbus, Ohio, and Columbia, South Carolina.

### Why Wasn't The New World Named After Columbus?

The names North and South America came about in a strange way. The continents were named after Amerigo Vespucci, an Italian who came along just a few years *after* Columbus. He happened to be in the right place at the right time. A German mapmaker named Ferdinand Waldseemuller first used the name America on a map he published in 1507. This was to honor Vespucci's discovery that South America was really a separate continent and not just a part of Asia.

# For Further Reading

Burnett, Bernice. *The First Book of Holidays*. Revised edition. New York: Franklin Watts, 1955, 1974.

Churchill, E. Richard. *Holiday Hullabaloo!* New York: Franklin Watts, 1977.

Grigoli, Valorie. *Patriotic Holidays and Celebrations. A First Book.* New York: Franklin Watts, 1985.

Heimann, Susan. *Christopher Columbus: A Visual Biography.* New York: Franklin Watts, 1973.

Ickis, Marguerite. *The Book of Patriotic Holidays.* New York: Dodd, Mead & Co., 1962.

Krythe, Maymie R. *All About American Holidays.* New York: Harper and Brothers, 1962.

Paulmier, Hilah and Robert Haven Schauffler (compilers and editors). *Columbus Day.* New York: Dodd, Mead and Co., 1938.

Sandak, Cass R. *Explorers and Discovery.* A First Reference Book. New York: Franklin Watts, 1983.

Sechrist, Elizabeth Hough. *Red Letter Days, A Book of Holiday Customs.* Revised edition. Philadelphia: Macrae Smith Company, 1940, 1965.

Soule, Gardner. *Christopher Columbus on the Green Sea of Darkness.* New York: Franklin Watts, 1988.

Sperry, Armstrong (author and illustrator). *The Voyages of Christopher Columbus.* A Landmark Book. New York: Random House, 1950.

# Index